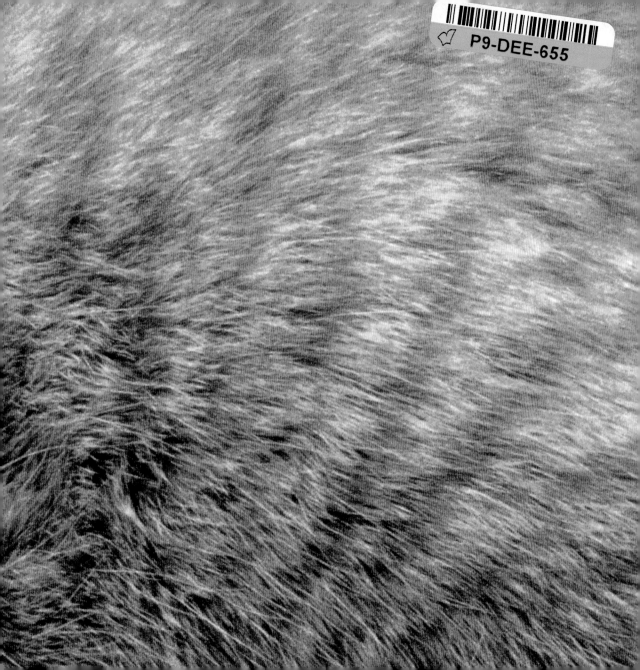

CATS
AT
WORK

By Rhonda Gray and Stephen T. Robinson

Commentary by Roger Caras

Commissioned Photography by Guy Powers

Abbeville Press · Publishers

New York · London · Paris

For Jordan and Troy.

Project editor: Susan Costello
Manuscript editor: Amy Handy
Designer: Renée Khatami
Production supervisor: Hope Koturo

Library of Congress
Cataloging-in-Publication Data
Gray, Rhonda.
    Cats at work / Rhonda Gray and Stephen T.
Robinson; commentary by Roger Caras.
        p. cm.
    ISBN 1-55859-153-2
    1. Working cats.   2. Working cats—
Pictorial works.   I. Robinson, Stephen T.
II. Caras, Roger A.   III. Title.
SF447.8.G73 1991
636.8—dc20   90-43286

Printed and bound in China.

First edition
10 9 8 7 6 5 4 3

This book is independent of *Working Cats*, by
Terry deRoy Gruber, and is not authorized by
the author thereof.

CONTENTS

TALE OF THE WORKING CAT

By Roger Caras

I t is generally believed that of all the animals man has truly domesticated—cat, dog, horse, ass (donkey, mule, and hinny), cow, zebu, pig, goat, sheep, the two camels (the one-humped kind and two-), llama and alpaca, yak, water buffalo or carabao, reindeer, honeybee, rabbit, guinea pig and other shelf pets, the various fowl both dry and wet, the smaller decorative birds, goldfish, guppies, mollies, koi and their kin, laboratory rats and mice, and fur animals like chinchilla, fox, and mink (heaven help them!)—the cat is about third from the bottom in *economic* value. Canaries and the like are at the very end of the list since we don't eat them or wear them, they don't carry messages, and we never stuff mattresses with their feathers. (Now that would be the ultimate orgy of hedonistic materialism—"Get your sleep on what used to peep.") And who ever heard of a guard canary? Hamsters, gerbils, and guinea pigs or cavies are down there, too, because they make very unsatisfactory beasts of burden and would be more likely to eat a warehouse than protect one.

The word *domesticated,* of course, means that at least some sort of genetic manipulation has been done somewhere along the line through selective breeding. That is why the working elephant, the moose, eland, vicuna, guanaco, musk-ox, trained cheetah, falcon, and the ferret or European stoat (that last one is a question-mark

"Types of cats," from Georges-Louis Leclerc de Buffon's Histoire naturelle, *late 18th century. Bibliothèque Nationale, Paris.*

species for this consideration, since it is uncertain whether any genetic manipulation occurred) don't make the real domestication list, although some of them have been in our service for a very long time. The concept of *domesticated* must never be confused with utilized, tamed, trained, or even socialized.

The yardstick of economic value is a strange one but we do tend to use it to the virtual exclusion of all others. It ignores the value of cats bought and sold (and plenty are), not to mention their undeniable value to the marketplace as consumers. The dollars' worth of canned, semimoist, and dry food, not to mention "treats," that they consume and the megabucks' worth of luxuries and presumed necessities like cushions, beds, domed and deodorized cat boxes, scratching posts and carpeted "apartment tree houses," litter, catnip and toys, sprays, combs, brushes, dry shampoos, vaccines, vitamins, flea collars, and airline crates—most of which are lovingly laid before them for approval—collectively amount to the GNP of each of several different nations in the Third World. Surely all of that is economic value of a kind, but, alas, that is not how that mysterious figure is reckoned. What is considered is that old all-too-human egocentric measure, *What have you done for me lately?*

And, indeed, what have cats done for us lately, or ever? Back to the beginning, or to what we tend to think we know or at least estimate may possibly have been the beginning. Man and some form of cat were apparently in association in very ancient times, maybe as far back as 7000 B.C., or so some graves near Jericho from prepottery times seem to suggest. But actual domestication in the sense of both possession and selective breeding? Give it to the Egyptians about 1600 B.C., the New Kingdom, eighteenth dynasty. Of course, no one chiseled into their diary, "Today, after lunch, we domesticated the cat." It may have happened around that time but it happened, we surmise, slowly. It wasn't a bolt-out-of-the-blue kind of thing, not at all; it was very much more an evolutionary process than that.

There was a neat and logical association that called for a domestic cat during that period. Man had just begun storing grain as a major economic undertaking. He had recently invented the silo to facilitate his efforts and that was a come-as-you-are invitation to rodents, of which the banks of the Nile have never been in short supply. A population explosion among rodents near human habitation—for that probably occurred—would have upgraded what then became a nice, unoccupied ecological niche. The cobras and other snakes surely moved in (followed by the mongoose) and so would have *Felis silvestris libyca,* the North African wildcat. In the ensuing millenia other forms of wildcats in other parts of the world may very well have contributed genes, colors, and coat textures to the domestic feline mix, but the cat that followed the rat in from the desert straight on into our hearts was in all likelihood off and running.

The cats newly in deep association with man were at work as soon as they arrived at the foot of the silo. They hit the ground running, so to speak. They worked out so well in those early

Foss dansant, *drawing by Edward Lear.*

centuries that they were promptly promoted to godhood. It was a crime punishable by death (probably not a pretty sight in ancient Egypt) to kill a cat, and when a cat died a natural death the people in its household (note *its,* a well-considered word in this context) were expected to shave their eyebrows. Tens of thousands of cats were transported to a special city, Bubastis, for mummification and burial after they had died. It is believed that there were some pretty neat orgies staged on and near the Nile to honor a cat-god named Bastet. The Egyptians really did take their hats off (and it seems a lot of other things, as well) to their little mousers in from the dunes.

What the economic worth of the emerging domestic cat was in comparison with the distinctly nondomesticated cobra as a hired gun in dynastic Egypt can never be calculated. It is enough to believe on good evidence that they did figure in. The cat helped, though; it did its job. It was certainly thanked.

After Egypt the cat's career was pretty checkered for a number of centuries. In Europe it fell from its pedestal with an awful thump. It was blamed for famine and plagues, while in fact it was clearly the only non–mumbo jumbo antiplague device working all through the Middle Ages. We know there were cats around farms, towns, cities, and villages, and they would naturally have hunted the rats that carried the plague-bearing fleas. We know pretty much how many people died of the plague—about a third of the population of Europe. What we do not know is how many people did not die of the plague because the cats did in the rats. We will in all likelihood never have an answer to that, of course, but it certainly must have been a factor.

Unfortunately for both man and cat, the relationship of the rat and the flea to the mounds of human corpses was not to be worked out for several centuries, so the cat never got deified again. The

Bronze sculpture of an Egyptian cat goddess, Late Dynastic period. The Metropolitan Museum of Art, New York; Purchase, 1958, Fund from Various Donors.

The Fortress of Cats, *medieval engraving from northern France. Bibliothèque Nationale, Paris.*

Cat taking part in a witches' Sabbath, painting from the studio of Hans Baldung-Grien. Photo courtesy of Giraudon/Art Resource.

people who survived didn't even thank them for their help. In fact, people continued to burn alive and otherwise discommode and discomfort the cat in diverse ways. It was not the best period in the cat's history. As the so-called familiar of witches, cats were fair game for every drunken lout in the town square. They were living soccer balls. The Protestants burned them to mock the Pope and the Catholics burned them to get even with the Protestants. The cats lost either way. The members of Islam were so angry about the Crusades they refused to play, and besides they had their own agenda. The Jews wisely kept out of it.

And so cats arrived in modern times, say from the eighteenth century on, carrying a great deal of historical baggage. Cardinals, poets, and artists loved them, while world-conquering, ''kneel at my feet'' types absolutely detested them. That has apparently always been the case. Among cats' worst detractors have been Napoleon Bonaparte and Adolph Hitler, who could not bear to be in the same room with them, and Alexander the Great, who reportedly fainted at the sight of one. Elizabeth I, a heavy-handed lady in her own regal way, was terrible to cats; if we are to believe history, she burnt them alive with her own hands. But we must never lose sight of the fact that history, as Emerson said, is a lie agreed upon. Nevertheless, people who need to conquer the world to make their day don't do well with the purring kind.

We have not elevated cats back to Olympian heights again, at least not yet, but they are back on the road to prereligious adoration in our time. And that brings us to another way of measuring worth or value. Psychiatrists and the like, explorers of motivation and the cybernetics of the mind, now say a nuzzling, silk-furred critter that seeks laps to purr in and demands attention to which it can respond with apparent love is very good for people. That is especially true in

Gustave Doré, ''Puss-in-Boots,'' illustration for Charles Perrault's fairy tales, 1862.

stressful times like these when alienation strikes down the innocent at a terrible rate. If cats are good medicine for loneliness and stress —and anyone who knows a cat knows they are—what is a cat worth? It is as difficult to put a dollar sign on that as it is to do a spreadsheet and find a "bottom line" for the flea-infested rats killed in Paris or London in the fifteenth century or evaluate the value in gold of the grain saved from mice and rats along the Nile during the infancy of the silo. Cats are imponderables, and that, I suspect— no, I *know*—is part of their charm.

Cats have been posing for paintings, friezes, statuary, and amulets since we and they began that early association in ancient Egypt. What do almost four thousand years of modeling fees add up to? They have also posed for thousands of poems, stories, tales, legends, and even modern novels. Virtually every category of creative mind has turned to them. A hit London and Broadway show called *Cats,* a character in *Peter and the Wolf* (the cat is personified by the clarinet), and many, many Japanese wood-block prints: cats, cats, and more cats. It is not just that cats posed or sat and were depicted and interpreted. No, far beyond that cats have *inspired* all of

Kuniyoshi, The Cat-Witch of Okabe, early- to mid-19th century. Victoria and Albert Museum, London.

John Tenniel, illustration of the Chesire Cat for Lewis Carroll's Alice in Wonderland.

Jean Baptiste Greuze, The Wool Winder, *1759. Copyright The Frick Collection, New York.*

that art literally for millenia. With French impressionist paintings approaching a hundred million dollars in the auction houses, what is the dollar value of inspiring almost four thousand years' worth of artists and craftsmen? What, in fact, is beauty worth and how do you measure it? What does it go for a pound or a yard or a peck?

If all of this possible aesthetic worth is vectored in with the number of people who may have survived the plague because of fewer rats and fleas, and with the amount of food salvaged because over nearly forty centuries literally billions of rats and mice didn't live to eat and procreate, how is it to be said that cats have little economic worth? Rubbish!

Take this scenario, which has quite probably been accurate on more than one occasion. Children are asleep upstairs in an old house. A mouse or rat quite intent on eating some more insulation off electrical wiring in the attic and triggering a potentially deadly fire stops off in the kitchen for a snack. On its rounds it spies a cracker left half-eaten on a plate on the kitchen table. The ever-hungry rodent goes for it and is spotted by the cat on duty nearby. The little beast dies and thereby does not get to eat the wiring. The fire doesn't start in the attic just over the heads of the sleeping children and whatever terrible things might have happened don't. Economic worth?

Morris the Cat at work. Courtesy of 9-Lives Cat Food. Photo courtesy of Daniel Edelman, Inc., Chicago.

This book is mostly about the things cats still do that are close to their original assignments. It is the work of two young people and it was clearly their goal to show their reverence, their respect, and their affection for a very good old idea, the domestic cat. I believe they have succeeded. They obviously had fun doing the job because it is fun seeing what they have done. In fact the whole thing, from idea to realization, is joyous, and that suits the cat and our relationship with such a lovely and loving being.

Cats always seem to be just hanging out. They don't lift that barge and tote that bale. That isn't their style. They are far too laid back. Few of them ever clown around as our equally beloved dogs do. No, cats hang around and when the opportunity arises they knock off a mouse here or a rat there, or they pose and offer a little inspiration to a poet or photographer, or they calm the odd frayed nerve and help a body fight an ulcer, stroke, or heart attack. All that is, as we said, somewhat difficult to quantify but so, then, is a mother's love for her child or a first baseman's love of the Game. One can say of the unmeasurable, be it love, the Game, or the cat, "It is and therefore it is excellent."

Felix the Cat, cartoon by Pat Sullivan.

NAME: kittens
SEX, AGE: hard to tell yet
BREED: American shorthairs
EMPLOYER: Bird store
"To teach the kittens not to mess with the inventory, we put them in with the big birds—Amazons, conures, and macaws—who bite their tails and pester them until they realize that chasing mice would be much more fun."

NAME: Lucky
SEX, AGE: Male, 7
BREED: American shorthair
EMPLOYER: The Humane Society of New York
"Lucky is a member of SAVE—Small Animal Visitors for the Elderly. He visits nursing home residents who can't have pets of their own."

NAME: Bianca
SEX, AGE: Female, 10 months
BREED: American shorthair
EMPLOYER: Pet supply store
"Bianca is always the center of attention. She not only has a nighttime fan club, but she insists on being a part of our window display."

NAME: Niké
SEX, AGE: Female, 8
BREED: American shorthair
EMPLOYER: Clothing designer and
hair stylist's studio
*"This little tuxedo is no slave
to fashion."*

NAME: Billie the Kittie
SEX, AGE: Female, 8
BREED: American shorthair
EMPLOYER: Lingerie store
*"When Billie the Kittie became too
Rubenesque to climb the stairs in my
apartment, I decided to give her a job
at the store. She fits in purrfectly."*

NAME: Shadow
SEX, AGE: Female, 2
BREED: American shorthair
EMPLOYER: Knitting factory
*"This cat's a troublemaker. Sometimes
when the girls come back from lunch,
they find that Shadow has unthreaded
their machines."*

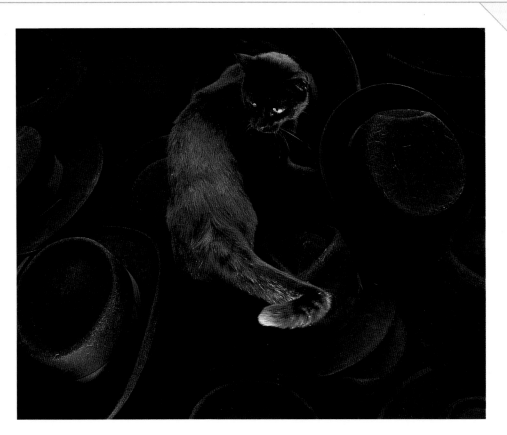

NAME: Samantha
SEX, AGE: Female, 5
BREED: American shorthair
EMPLOYER: New York Shakespeare
Festival, costume shop
"Samantha is a real perfectionist. In the morning we find all her mice lined up neatly in a row."

NAME: Elizabeth
SEX, AGE: Male, 1
BREED: Domestic shorthair
EMPLOYER: Hat factory
"Our cats have, on several occasions, become enclosed in a hatbox and readied for shipping. We've now instituted a last 'cat check' before we let the boxes leave the warehouse."

NAME: Alice
SEX, AGE: Female, 8
BREED: American shorthair
EMPLOYER: Antique clothing store
*"If you come into the store with
children, Alice will 'babysit' with them
while you shop."*

NAME: Pancho
SEX, AGE: Male, 8
BREED: Abyssinian mix
EMPLOYER: Antique store
*"Pancho is such a neighborhood
celebrity that he actually lures
customers into the store. He's been
very good for business."*

NAME: Tasha, Regina, Mommy Cat,
and Poto
SEX, AGE: Females, 8, 3, 6, and 3
BREED: Burmese, Siamese mix,
American shorthairs
EMPLOYER: Clothing store
*"All our cats wear shoplifting sensors
to prevent them from wandering
outside."*

NAME: Kitty Boy
SEX, AGE: Male, 10
BREED: American shorthair
EMPLOYER: Boutique
*"Kitty Boy wandered in seven years
ago during a blizzard and he
never left."*

NAME: Heidi and Henry
SEX, AGE: Female, 4; male, 5
BREED: American shorthairs
EMPLOYER: Antique store
*"If Heidi and Henry are the king and
queen of this store, they have
many thrones."*

NAME: Jesse
SEX, AGE: Male, 4
BREED: American shorthair
EMPLOYER: Cat specialty store
"I'll never forget the time Jesse was asleep in a basket full of stuffed animals. A customer tried to pick him up by his tail and nearly had a heart attack. . . . Jesse nearly had one, too."

NAME: FICA
SEX, AGE: Male, 5
BREED: Himalayan
EMPLOYER: Dance studio
*"This gorgeous cat appeared on the
day the Federal Insurance
Contributions Act was due . . . and
that explains why we named
him FICA."*

NAME: Flex
SEX, AGE: Male, 3
BREED: American shorthair
EMPLOYER: Piano teacher/tuner's studio
*"Though he's not generally allowed
inside the grand pianos, Flex
sometimes sneaks in while I'm playing.
He loves to chase the hammers as they
hit the strings."*

NAME: Groucho
SEX, AGE: Male, 1
BREED: American shorthair
EMPLOYER: Drum studio
*"Groucho is our Percussive Kitty
Extraordinaire."*

NAME: Goonie
SEX, AGE: Female, 6
BREED: American shorthair
EMPLOYER: Recording studio
*"Goonie really keeps us on our toes
when she's in the studio during a
recording session. She's been known
to walk across the sound board,
pushing buttons and altering the mix
of the recording."*

NAME: Pussifica T. Cat
SEX, AGE: Male, 12
BREED: American shorthair
EMPLOYER: Radio station
*"Pussifica is licensed by the FCC
as a third-class radio operator."*

NAME: Vladimir
SEX, AGE: Male, 2
BREED: Siamese mix
EMPLOYER: Record store
"Vladimir's the coolest."

NAME: Tomato
SEX, AGE: Female, 4
BREED: American shorthair
EMPLOYER: Guitar store
*"Whenever I play one of the guitars
Tomato will paw at the strings, making
for some pretty interesting
arrangements of some otherwise
standard tunes."*

NAME: Cue
SEX, AGE: Female, 8
BREED: Siamese
EMPLOYER: Billiards hall
"Cue racks up lots of time on our tables."

NAME: Katrick
SEX, AGE: Male, 22
BREED: American shorthair
and ocelot mix
EMPLOYER: Antique toy dealer
"Katrick is rumored to be the great-grandson of an ocelot and a tom cat."

NAME: Grace
SEX, AGE: Female, 9
BREED: American shorthair
EMPLOYER: Chess club
"Some of the best chess players in the world come here to play. Grace is nice to have around for the most part, but she has been known to upset some pretty intense games."

NAME: Cleo
SEX, AGE: Male, 3
BREED: American shorthair
EMPLOYER: Pinball-machine dealer
*"Cleo has such a funny personality
that sometimes I think we should have
named him 'Tilt.'"*

NAME: Woody and Risky
SEX, AGE: Males, 10 and 13
BREED: Manx and Siamese
EMPLOYER: Card and gift store
"Woody and Risky work hard . . . at
drawing attention to themselves."

NAME: Blax
SEX, AGE: Male, 4
BREED: American shorthair
EMPLOYER: Party goods store
*"Blax is constantly trying to improve
our window displays."*

NAME: Maxie
SEX, AGE: Female, 1
BREED: Russian Blue
EMPLOYER: Dried flower specialty store
"To watch Maxie move among the dried flower arrangements, you'd think she knows how delicate they are."

NAME: Boris
SEX, AGE: Male, 2
BREED: American shorthair
EMPLOYER: Florist
"We found Boris and some other stray kittens under the grandstands at the 1988 U.S. Tennis Open in Forest Hills, New York. He's named after Becker, of course."

NAME: Amber
SEX, AGE: Female, 16
BREED: Persian
EMPLOYER: Bar and restaurant
"Amber is the perfect hostess. She's very attentive—especially if you've ordered crab or shrimp!"

NAME: Dirty Harry and Taka
SEX, AGE: Male, 6; female, 8
BREED: American shorthairs
EMPLOYER: Deli
"These cats often disappear during the day to roam the neighborhood, but they're never gone long enough to miss their dinner."

NAME: Miss Roger
SEX, AGE: Female, 12
BREED: American shorthair
EMPLOYER: Restaurant

"One day an actor was sitting at a table near the window. Miss Roger joined him, and a crowd of people gathered to gawk. The actor thought they were looking at him. Miss Roger knew they were looking at her. She was right!"

NAME: Myra
SEX, AGE: Female, 4
BREED: American shorthair
EMPLOYER: Café
*"Myra's necklace was a gift from
one of her customers."*

NAME: Pancho
SEX, AGE: Male, 1
BREED: American shorthair
EMPLOYER: Kitchen-supply store
"If this nutty little cat is not sleeping on the marble countertops or in a pot (!), he's snoozing in one of the comfy linen cabinets."

NAME: Susie
SEX, AGE: Female, 2
BREED: American shorthair
EMPLOYER: Market
"Susie's a tough little cat. She doesn't care what breed, size, or shape a dog is —if it's in her store, it's fair game."

NAME: Puss
SEX, AGE: Male, 11
BREED: American shorthair
EMPLOYER: Gourmet coffee-bean shop
"Comfort he's familiar with. But when it comes to coffee, Puss doesn't know beans."

NAME: Spike
SEX, AGE: Female, 6
BREED: American shorthair
EMPLOYER: Bakery
"Spike is not pure-bread."

NAME: Pablo
SEX, AGE: Male, 3
BREED: American shorthair
EMPLOYER: Deli
*"Pablo will play with anyone who
will play with him."*

NAME: Peewee and Buster
SEX, AGE: Males, 6
BREED: American shorthairs
EMPLOYER: Spice shop
*"Peewee and Buster allow me to
dress them up on holidays. For
Halloween, Peewee is a mouse and
Buster is the devil. At Christmas,
Peewee dresses as the old woman in
'The Night before Christmas.' For
Easter, they both wear bunny ears."*

NAME: Novi
SEX, AGE: Male, 4
BREED: American shorthair
EMPLOYER: Pasta shop and restaurant
*"Novi's name fits his personality—it's
short for Casanova."*

NAME: Tina
SEX, AGE: Female, 2
BREED: American shorthair
EMPLOYER: Wine store
*"Sometimes Tina goes home with us
—I guess that makes her a part-time
working cat."*

NAME: Minnie
SEX, AGE: Female, 12
BREED: American shorthair
EMPLOYER: Pizzeria
*"If Minnie is not around when we're
closing up, no one is permitted to
leave until we find her."*

NAME: Charlie
SEX, AGE: Male, 10
BREED: American shorthair
EMPLOYER: Candy store
"Charlie's favorite place to sleep is right next to the KitKat bars."

NAME: Mr. Bigelow
SEX, AGE: Male, 10
BREED: American shorthair
EMPLOYER: Pharmacy
*"There might be a dozen people
waiting for a chair, but if Mr. Bigelow
is sleeping in it, they all know they'll
have to stand."*

NAME: Perdue and Bunny
SEX, AGE: Male, 7; female, 3
BREED: American shorthairs
EMPLOYER: Floor-sanding equipment
rental shop
*"Perdue and Bunny are known as
'The Exterminators.'"*

NAME: Nicer
SEX, AGE: Male, 12
BREED: Siamese mix
EMPLOYER: Hardware and
housewares store
*"The store originally adopted another
cat from the same litter but gave it
back—this one was 'Nicer.'"*

NAME: Pussy Cat
SEX, AGE: Female, 8
BREED: American shorthair
EMPLOYER: Laundromat
"I just call her 'The Boss.'"

NAME: Tiger
SEX, AGE: Male, 2
BREED: American shorthair
EMPLOYER: Shoe repair shop
"If mice or dogs enter Tiger's shop, they can expect to get the boot."

NAME: Fufu
SEX, AGE: Male, 3
BREED: American shorthair
EMPLOYER: Electric-motor repair shop
*"Fufu is rarely seen in the shop—he
prefers to spend his time in the office
. . . watching TV."*

NAME: Willie
SEX, AGE: Female, 2
BREED: Russian Blue
EMPLOYER: Locksmith/
sewing-machine repair shop
*"Willie is enchanting. It's her job
to entertain our customers if they
have to wait."*

NAME: Offset
SEX, AGE: Male, 5
BREED: American shorthair
EMPLOYER: Printing company
*"Offset loves to lie on the hot stacks
after they've come out of the printer,
'offsetting' the job, which is how he
got his name."*

NAME: Miss Cat
SEX, AGE: Female, 4
BREED: American shorthair
EMPLOYER: Iron workshop
"Miss Cat wears a collection of dirt and metal shavings that goes back some fifty-six years. When I can't find her, I just take out a magnet!"

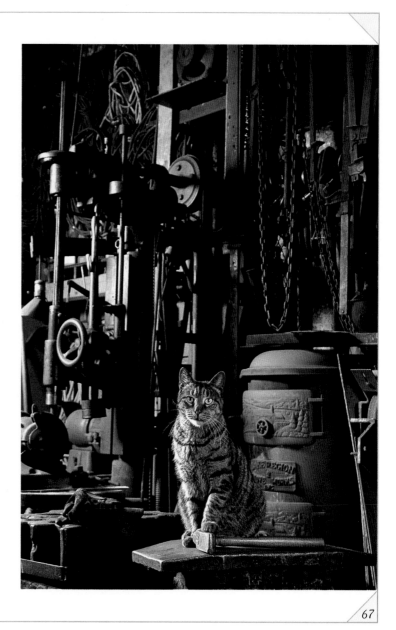

NAME: Negrita
SEX, AGE: Female, 4
BREED: American shorthair
EMPLOYER: Copy shop
*"Negrita has a friend named Molly
who comes in every day to play with
her and give her a little catnip."*

NAME: Mayday
SEX, AGE: Male, 2
BREED: American shorthair
EMPLOYER: Graphic design studio
*"One day, while sitting on the warm
copy machine, Mayday managed to
photocopy his rear end."*

NAME: Mandu
SEX, AGE: Male, 4
BREED: Blue Point Siamese
EMPLOYER: Record company
"Mandu won't listen to audition tapes and he has never signed a new band, but he does relieve stress—he always seems to know who's lap needs him the most."

NAME: Be Be
SEX, AGE: Female, 2
BREED: American shorthair
EMPLOYER: Public relations firm
"Be Be's very technically inclined and loves to work on the computer, the answering machine, and the adding machine, not to mention the telephone, the photocopier. . . ."

NAME: Boomis
SEX, AGE: Male, 1
BREED: American shorthair
EMPLOYER: Movie theater
*"Once Boomis was playing with a
mouse in the front row, casting
shadows on the screen that many in
the audience thought was part of the
movie. He also likes to jump in our
patrons' laps, which can scare them—
especially if they've never met Boomis."*

NAME: Datchery
SEX, AGE: Male, 5
BREED: American shorthair
EMPLOYER: Producer Joseph
Papp's office
*"I think there's a little actor in
Datchery. He never misses an
opportunity to cross the stage during
a reading."*

NAME: Bill, Baby, Big Kitty,
and Hannah
SEX, AGE: Females, ages unknown
BREED: American shorthairs; Persian
EMPLOYER: Sculptor's studio
*"With so many places to hide in a
studio this big, there's almost no
chance that you'll see more than one
or two cats at the same time."*

NAME: Suky
SEX, AGE: Female, 3
BREED: American shorthair
EMPLOYER: Exotic jewelry
and gems store
"Suky is our most precious gem."

NAME: Max
SEX, AGE: Male, 9
BREED: American shorthair
EMPLOYER: New York Shakespeare
Festival, props department
"Though Max has never performed in anything written by Shakespeare, he has, on occasion, shown up next door at the Astor Place Theater—on stage, during a performance."

NAME: Punky
SEX, AGE: Female, 15
BREED: American shorthair
EMPLOYER: Plastics supply company
*"Two other cats work in the store, but
Punky would rather play amongst her
large plastic friends."*

NAME: Luci
SEX, AGE: Female, 5
BREED: American shorthair
EMPLOYER: Lighting fixtures store
"The neatest thing about Luci is that she loves to sing to the pigeons."

NAME: José
SEX, AGE: Male, 12
BREED: American shorthair
EMPLOYER: Loftbed and futon store
"José does such a good job keeping rodents away that sometimes he will go out, catch one, and bring it back to the store to play with."

NAME: Huey
SEX, AGE: Male, 3
BREED: American shorthair
EMPLOYER: Photographer's studio
"Huey's such a ham! Whenever I'm setting up for a shoot, he comes around. The minute the lights go on, he's posing."

NAME: Zinny
SEX, AGE: Male, 11
BREED: American shorthair
EMPLOYER: Frame store
*"We couldn't picture this place
without Zinny."*

NAME: Madison
SEX, AGE: Female, 3
BREED: American shorthair
EMPLOYER: Antique poster store
"Madison gets along great with the neighborhood dogs—as long as there's a window between them."

NAME: Tex
SEX, AGE: Male, 12
BREED: American shorthair
EMPLOYER: T-shirt shop
"In T-shirt lingo, Tex is what you'd call an XXL."

NAME: Kate
SEX, AGE: Female, 10
BREED: American shorthair
EMPLOYER: Chess bookstore
"Kate 2, Rodents 0."

NAME: Thorton, Mitchell, and Christopher
SEX, AGE: Males, 2, 5, and 13
BREED: American shorthairs; Maine coon and Persian mix
EMPLOYER: 20th-century literature bookseller

"As far as these cats are concerned, great literature is judged by its cover: Just how comfortable is it to sleep on?"

NAME: Mimi
SEX, AGE: Female, 3
BREED: American shorthair
EMPLOYER: Art book and card store
"Mimi defected from a restaurant down the street. We fell in love with her and granted her permanent asylum."

NAME: Ms. Q
SEX, AGE: Female, 12
BREED: Siamese mix
EMPLOYER: Comic-book store
"Ms. Q is not a very good mouser— she does a much better job keeping dogs out of the store."

NAME: Program
SEX, AGE: Male, 5
BREED: American shorthair
EMPLOYER: Self-help bookstore
"Having a cat like Program around is great therapy."

NAME: Carlito
SEX, AGE: Male, 8 months
BREED: American shorthair
EMPLOYER: Bicycle shop
"Carlito was raised by our dog. He sleeps with the dog and eats the dog's food—I don't think he knows he's a cat."

NAME: Good Boy
SEX, AGE: Male, 5
BREED: American shorthair
EMPLOYER: Health food and
vitamin store
*"Good Boy may seem a bit large to
some, but we consider him 'healthy.'"*

NAME: Cat
SEX, AGE: Female, 4
BREED: American shorthair
EMPLOYER: NYPD, 6th Precinct,
Detectives' Squad
*"Cat caught eighteen mice in her first
two weeks on the job. The cops
downstairs tried to get her to work for
them, but she can't be bribed."*

NAME: Charlie
SEX, AGE: Male, 4
BREED: American shorthair
EMPLOYER: NYFD, Ladder 21,
Engine Co. 34
"We rescued Charlie from a fire when he was a kitten. His job is to catch an occasional mouse, and he's even joined us on some of our calls."

NAME: Angel One
(Angel Two on patrol)
SEX, AGE: Male, 3; female, 3
BREED: American shorthairs
EMPLOYER: Guardian Angels
safety patrol
*"Angel One and Angel Two are the
rodent patrol. They are the guardian
angels of the Guardian Angels."*

ACKNOWLEDGMENTS

The authors wish to thank all the business owners and their employees (furry and otherwise), without whose time and assistance this book would not have been possible. We would also like to express our appreciation to all those at Abbeville Press involved with this project, especially Amy Handy, Susan Costello, and Renée Khatami, for their patience and creative vision. Thanks to Carl Jacobs for his support and to Roger Caras, who elevated this book to another level. Special thanks to those working cats whose businesses didn't make it through a tough editing process.

Most especially, the authors wish to thank their parents, Jeanne and Larry Gray, Helen Robinson, and the late James R. Robinson, DVM.

INDEX

Front of jacket: Huey (see page 80)
Back of jacket: Zinny (see page 81)

Page 1: NAME: Mommy and Daddy
SEX, AGE: Female, 3; male, 3
BREED: American shorthairs
EMPLOYER: Office furniture store
*"Mommy and Daddy sleep all day.
They work the night shift."*

Pages 2–3: NAME: Matilda
SEX, AGE: Female, 4
BREED: American shorthair
EMPLOYER: Algonquin Hotel
*"Matilda is the princess of the Algonquin.
Her bed and toys are in the lobby and her
commissioned portrait hangs over the bar."*

Pages 4–5: Victoria and Elizabeth (see page 25)

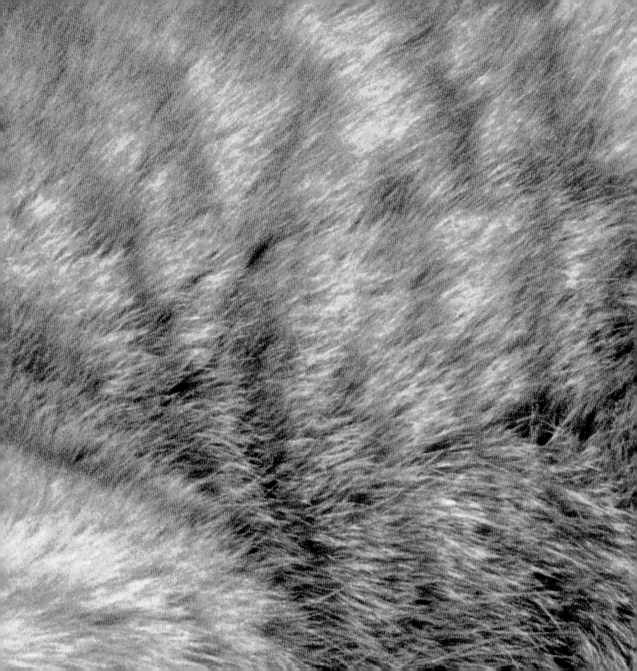